# ABOUT THAT DAY

## TASHA MALCOLM

Fulton Books
Meadville, PA


Published by Fulton Books 2024


ISBN 979-8-89427-721-9 (paperback)
ISBN 979-8-89427-722-6 (digital)


Printed in the United States of America

# PREFACE

This memoir is dedicated to all brothers and sisters-in-arms. This memoir reflects my personal experiences as an African American, single mom, baby boomer, and female soldier in the US Army. I served from December 1, 1982, to May 1, 2005. The events described in this memoir occurred in preparation for and during my first deployment to Iraq. My eight-month deployment began on May 7, 2003, until January 18, 2004. I was medically evacuated and returned to my duty station in Germany due to an asthma attack in Baghdad on January 17, 2004.

I feel all soldiers borne of war during this era have fallen through the voids for VA care, to include treatment for the various mental health conditions we all suffer from, the absence of face-to-face therapy vs video mental health appointments, suffering mental anguish alone, physical wounds without a cure, and our refusal to fit in a VA medical box. Doctor's notes describe many combat veterans as combative; instead, I prefer to say we are *not* combative; instead, we are more often misunderstood. This is an opportunity to portray the daily challenges, the living conditions, the total absence of plumbing (except at the mobile shower point), along with the systemic yet subtle abuses of military culture. Boarding a plane to an unknown destination unleashed a myriad of emotions and questions that I will address.

I would like all military and veteran comrades to know how oak-tree strong and resilient we are, regardless of adverse and traumatic events we have been faced with. This determination extends to our post-military service. Use every breath to encourage and uplift yourself and all who served, regardless of our fear and trauma; we must be there for each other and continue to *drive on* as we were trained to do.

My trauma recovery is not over and has been nothing less than a constant struggle post-combat. Trying to figure out what works and what doesn't regarding treatment and therapy. I have leaned heavily on my Christian faith, parental training, military training, and vast life experiences. I use this particular recipe of acquired strength for everyday encouragement and mental survival. Some days, it is a struggle to get out of bed due to mental and physical health challenges. Feeling like no one understands makes these burdens of war even more important. What we carry daily in our rucksack is immense. The rucksack needs to be repacked frequently to lighten the accumulation of everyday triggers. This prevents our rucksack from being too large and heavy to carry. Your lives are important; please don't think about the alternative. As comrades in arms, we must find a way to draw from other strengths when we feel too weak and overwhelmed. Surround yourself with like-minded people or soldier friends, and find love where it's true. When love is no longer being served, leave that table. Don't compromise with domestic violence. Straighten up your crown, build your own table, and serve love as a buffet item. I am working on my third divorce and can't seem to get it right in relationships. This is a direct result of PTSD and undiagnosed brain trauma.

My heart is with all of you, no matter how tattered, weathered, or scraped up, and with all your visible and nonvisible wounds of war. You are forever *beautiful* and *loved*, regardless of your sexual orientation.

Treat every day with appreciation, and remember to respect yourselves. Self-respect becomes the manual for how others should treat you.

Tasha

# CHAPTER 1

On April 9, 2003, an interruption from regularly scheduled programming occurred on the Armed Forces Network (AFN). I was finishing my lunch in the break room of our office at Wiesbaden Airbase, Germany. Accompanied by two coworkers: Master Sergeant Jefferson and Mr. Pelko (a government civilian employee), we watched in awe as the statue of Saddam Hussein was being toppled over by US soldiers. This televised show of force confirmed that the "splat had hit the fan." I knew to get my life in order swiftly.

According to the official Iraq timeline, "the invasion of Iraq" began on March 19, 2003, and lasted until President Bush declared the end of combat operations on May 1, 2003. My armored division landed in Camp Arifjan, Kuwait, on May 8, 2003. The US-led coalition and our allies performed jointly to overtake Saddam's Army and to disarm

Iraq of "weapons of mass destruction." President Bush considered the end of combat operations a victory. Nevertheless, our country entered a ten-year war with 4,432 reported American fatalities. War involves the loss of life, which saddens me. Soldiers whose lives were lost before they were of legal age to drink deepen my sadness.

Deploying for the first time and being of such maturity, this fact shook me every day. I was considerably older than the average soldier when I was called to fight. I had turned forty in March 2003 before departing for Iraq in May, was serving my nineteenth year of active duty, and had accumulated twenty-one years of service.

My Army career began when I joined the US Army Reserves in April 1982. My first duty station was the US Army Reserve Center in St. Louis, Missouri. I served with this unit from April 1983 to October 1984. My first military occupational specialty (MOS) was 62B (Heavy Construction Equipment Repair). Why did I choose this MOS? I scored high for mechanical aptitude on the Armed Services Vocational Aptitude Battery (ASVAB)! Even though my entire work history was secretarial.

Thankfully, achieving academic excellence while in high school was one path that equated to eternal independence. My guidance counselor was also my chemistry teacher, and I was one of the few students who stayed awake during chemistry class. That class was on the third floor of my school; I would sit by the window if I turned catacorner, and I would watch strung-out heroin addicts shoot up alongside the exterior wall of the apartment building diagonally on the corner during chemistry class. That was further demonstration of how *my* life would *not* be.

In June 1979, at the end of my junior year and entering my senior year, my life became horribly skewed. I became pregnant. There were two times my guidance counselor saved my bacon. The first day of my senior year, she was the first person I made an appointment with.

After telling her about my irresponsible summer, we decided it would be best for me to attend Saint Margaret's School for unwed mothers in Dorchester, Massachusetts, and she would send my schoolwork weekly. I worked self-paced from October 1979 until I rejoined my class two weeks after the birth of my daughter on March 17, 1980. In the same month I gave birth, I also turned seventeen. I can proudly say I marched with my class on June 6, 1980, at the Prudential Center in downtown Boston.

I appreciated my mother's wisdom in knowing Massachusetts had the best public and college prep schools compared to E. St. Louis, Illinois, where I grew up. I was allowed to live with my granny. Since I arrived in March of 1977, I had to enroll at Boston High School, where I began freshman high school near downtown Boston. The following year, I began my sophomore year at James E. Barry High School in Dorchester, where I lived.

The second time my chemistry teacher/guidance counselor saves my bacon is when I was offered the opportunity to work at the MECH Corporation in Bedford, Massachusetts. The MECH Corp. works in conjunction with Hanscom AFB to build planes for the US Air Force. I received a permanent job offer after working with them during spring break of my senior year, 1980. I was a secretary for a team of ten engineers. It was a very interesting job; however, I had a lot on my plate at that time. I was an ill-equipped seventeen-year-old teenage mom. If it weren't for my grandmother and twin sisters, who lived in Dorchester, and my guidance counselor, who never gave up on me, motherhood would have been a real disaster. I received a nursing scholarship at the prestigious Northwestern University in Evanston, Illinois, following graduation. Yet I felt that being a young mother would prevent my shot at attending college. The scholarship was great, but the cost of living would have been impossible without a job. I felt as though working and attending nursing school would have been a recipe for failure. I envisioned that the pressure of being a mom in addition to attending college would be more than I could handle. Trying to make the right decision at this point brought about depression. I didn't know what depression was until many years later.

Shortly after graduating, I accepted the job at MECH. I was so relieved; I would work and earn money to support my child and have a place of my own. Even so, I was still unable to financially support myself and a young child on my own. After two years of working, I resigned my job at MECH and went back to my parents in Illinois to look for work closer to my aging parents. Jobs were not very lucrative in Illinois. In Boston, I could get jobs any day of the week, although the wages were always at the bottom of the scale.

I joined the Army a few months after returning to Illinois, with an almost immediate departure of two weeks after being sworn in. My child remained in Boston with my grandparents. I felt a reprieve when I joined, and since I had a bit of experience with the reserve unit, I was a specialist fourth-class (E4) when I left the reserve component. Once I transferred to active duty, I later found out that only active-duty rank is transferable, so I lost all rank received in the Army reserves. Through grit and determination, I did regain all my rank within six months. Every rank I earned came with two waivers: time in grade and time in service, allowing me to become a SP4 the same year of arrival, 1984. Completing Army correspondence courses became my strategy to accumulate an extensive amount of promotion points, which helped me make SGT/E5. Medical correspondence courses held the biggest points. Therefore, that is where I started. I had a trunk full of correspondence courses in the event of downtime, such as appointments, especially during twenty-four-hour duty. I would finish courses like I was the third monkey trying to get on Noah's ark in the rain.

I maximized all points for correspondence courses. I was allowed to attend the SGT/E5 board in September 1984 and was promoted to a non-commissioned officer effective December 1, 1985, which was astonishing to me. My child joined me at my first duty station in Mainz, Germany, in 1984. Life was still a struggle, as I was residing off-post in the German economy. Living on the economy was more expensive than living in government housing on the base. I had to pay rent in deutsche marks, and our cost-of-living benefit was always one month in arrears. I didn't receive any housing stipends for my dependent child for two years. Your family is what determines the amount of the housing stipend. When I did receive my back pay, it was in the amount of $10,000. I owed the majority to my wonderful German landlord, Herr Schmidt, who never gave me a hard time about not being able to pay rent. My daughter and I slept with sweats on every night in the winter because using heat in Germany was financial suicide. Germany taught me how to be mindful about spending, and I learned to sustain myself and my child through the turbulence of being a single mom while serving my country.

# CHAPTER 2

**D**uring the war in Iraq, the average active-duty soldier's age ranged from seventeen to thirty-two. I turned forty in March 2003, two months before departing for Iraq in May 2003. I was serving my nineteenth year of active duty and had accumulated twenty-one years of service. Deploying for the first time and being of such maturity is a fact that shook me every day. I was considerably older than the average soldier when I was called to punch my ticket on the battlefield.

Soldiers from my division received our deployment orders on April 16, 2003, seven days following the fall of Saddam's statue. The division's departure date was May 7, 2003; the return date was *"indefinite."* During that moment, I was writing a blank selfless check with my life in exchange for my country's freedom against terror. It was time to do what I signed up and trained for. I was painfully aware of the real possibility of not returning to my family at all or not being the same as when I left. I was ready to go and fight for my country and flag against terrorism. The reality of what could happen to the US in the post-9/11 days prepared me to fly to an unknown destination and fight for freedoms against all enemies, "foreign and domestic." This statement is a blurb taken from swearing the oath of enlistment.

I loosely compare joining the military to being in the Mafia. You take an oath like the Omerta, the Italian Mafia code of honor. Violating the oath of enlistment can cause almost the same consequences in the military as in the Mafia. The difference between the two is that a soldier's death may not be as instantaneous as with the Mafia.

Several of my family members had joined the Army, so I wasn't at all apprehensive or fearful of enlisting. My uncle Herman enlisted in the Merchant Marines, both of his sons enlisted in the Marine Corps, and my older cousin Pete completed four years in the Army. Pete was my idol. I joined in 1982 at the age of twenty-two years old. My cousin Pete came to the hotel before I left for basic training, and we had a necessary talk about the dos and don'ts. He told me to never volunteer for anything and don't hang out with the problematic soldiers. In other words, keep your nose clean. After researching the five military services, I decided the Army best suited me. I can't swim, ruling out the Navy, Marines, and Coast Guard. So the Army and Air Force were my two choices because of my inability to swim. The Air Force was a little too inflexible for me. I really liked the variety the Army offered; I could later change my MOS if I desired. I changed my MOS as a first reenlistment option. I reenlisted from Heavy Construction Equipment Repair to the Adjutant General's Corps. My job became 75B Standard Installation and Division Personnel Reporting Systems (SIDPERS) clerk, performing personnel and administrative functions during my various units of assignment.

Becoming a sergeant didn't solidify the Army as a career for me until I wanted to end my term of service and join the Pennsylvania State Police during my tenth year of enlistment. I sought out this opportunity for a more stable life for my child, who became a tween in middle school while living at the New Susquehanna Army Depot in Pennsylvania. My duty station, however, was a forty-five-minute drive up Interstate 81 North to Fort Discover Gap in the city of Saint. Also known as the "Gap," this base is the State National Guard headquarters.

When I decided to apply to the PA State Police, there was an age discrimination lawsuit actively being litigated for PA State Police applicants over the age of twenty-six years old. I was thirty years old at the time, and my application would have been rejected. I couldn't wait for this lawsuit to be adjudicated because there is a certain window in which you must reenlist.

Becoming a PA State trooper was foiled, so I continued my service in the Army until retirement. Following the assignment in Pennsylvania, I was subsequently assigned to the 18th Airborne Corps at Fort Bragg, North Carolina, with duty in Cairo, Egypt, from June 1995 to December 1997. I was stationed at the Cairo Embassy, with duty in a suburb called Maadi. The lovely thing about administration as an MOS is that you can be assigned anywhere with any unit. In Cairo, I was assigned to a M1A1 tank unit, which helped the Egyptian Land Forces Army integrate M1A1 tanks into their arsenal and with how to maintain them. Maadi, a suburb of Cairo, is six miles from the American Embassy, and during traffic, this ten-minute drive easily turned into forty-five minutes of horn-blowing insanity. I must say it was always exciting to see the goings-on out the window of my vehicle—every day was filled with excitement, and you never knew what you would witness. I was awestruck seeing the daily rituals of Egyptians: if there is a religious holiday coming up, you can see cows being slaughtered on the sidewalk, blood everywhere.

There is a lesson Americans learn upon arrival: if you go into a meat market and there are no flies on the meat, versus a meat market with flies on the meat, which meat market should you choose? No flies mean there is insecticide on the meat. Go with the flies; the meat is natural and safe. I would pick my live chicken out at the meat market, and a cut and cleaned chicken would be delivered to my house.

My primary personnel duties were arranging incoming and outgoing personnel. The importance of the personnel mission is to never have a disproportionate number of assigned soldiers. I managed the logistics of bringing incoming personnel and their families into their quarters and moving departing personnel from their assigned quarters to transition quarters, awaiting their transfer back to stateside assignments. I was the sole personnel and mail clerk for my eleven-person unit. Everyone had to be in possession of a government credit card. My responsibility monthly was to ensure the purchases on that card were authorized transactions. I worked right next door to my apartment. I reported to work at 8:00 a.m.; my priorities were to receive gasoline receipts from Mr. Mohammed, the supervisor of the ten drivers, ensure the figures were correct, and place them in my reimbursement folder, to be reimbursed by the American Embassy's finance office. I was responsible for two thousand EGP (Egyptian pounds), the maximum amount of my petty cash.

I ensured there was always the exact amount on hand in the event of a necessary purchase on the local economy. At 11:30 a.m., I was driven to the embassy by my assigned driver, Nagib. Every day, we went a different way to avert a possible terrorist attack. Nagib was a forty-year-old driver who was married with two sons, also known as Giba to us, and the other ten drivers were the best friends we had; they were responsible for our safety and cultural intelligence, and every morning they brought our breakfast. Ironically, against cultural norms, the men ate with the women only at work. Outside of work, this would have been deemed inappropriate. Our drivers taught us the dos and don'ts of Egyptian culture and mannerism. There are vitally important Egyptian cultural norms, such as: don't ever cross your legs and reveal the soles of your feet or the palms of your hands. The soles of your feet should only be seen after death. This is a biggie: people freak out at the way Americans cross their legs horizontally, resting your leg on your opposite thigh. They mumble prayers and immediately vacate the room. Your palms facing anyone is simply impolite; Americans signal "come here" by an open palm and fingers motioning toward you. The culturally correct way in Egypt is, the palm is facing the ground with fingers motioning toward you.

Men and unmarried women are not to go out in public without an escort. The marriage of daughters is a financial escalation for the members of her family. The woman's father has stock in her purity and can demand a very high dowry. A young woman who is found to have lost her virginity in Egypt is a death sentence for her. By way of honor killing, she risks being murdered by her father, brother, or uncles; this was fully acceptable during my time there. It was not uncommon for these customs to be strictly adhered to and vehemently enforced without question.

The success of my day was to follow a strict schedule of where I had to be and what needed to be done. To maximize time, I incorporated mail distribution with my lunch at 1:00 p.m. to 2:30 p.m. The mail room was on the top floor of our residential building. Our workweek began on Sunday to

Thursday. Friday was the Muslim day of prayer at the mosque.

I enjoyed playing softball. Friday, Saturday, and Sunday—we play for ten hours on these days. Personal cars were shipped to Egypt at the government's expense, allowing individuals or groups to travel to most parts of the country. After receiving my Egyptian driver's license, I often traveled to the Red Sea and the pyramids, meeting and bonding with people who are still my friends since my arrival in 1995.

Unfortunately, Egypt was a twenty-four-month tour; I extended my tour by six months to a thirty-month tour. In December 1995, my daughter, Miriam, was sixteen years old when she traveled to Egypt for Christmas. I took her to the Cairo Opera House to see the *Nutcracker*.

When the permanent change of station came, I decided to reenlist for the maximum four-year commitment. At this time, I am in my fourteenth year. My follow-up assignment after Cairo was Fort McCain, Arizona. This move was appealing because the weather was akin to Egypt.

Unfortunately, when I arrived in January 1998, there was an El Niño in effect, and I developed pneumonia and was admitted to the hospital. My new first sergeant and his daughter welcomed me to the unit while I was still in the hospital.

While assigned to this unit, I discovered a sergeant first class (SFC) who did not have an effective department of the Army promotion order for that rank. I hunted and checked, only to find out that the soldier was fraudulently wearing a higher rank than was authorized. The soldier's previous duty station was investigated for manufacturing fake high school diplomas to recruit soldiers. The soldier accrued a military debt for money owed to the defense and finance office while she deceptively pretended to have attained this SFC/E7 rank.

A few months later, I was promoted to sergeant first class at Fort McCain on October 1, 1998. Upon being promoted, I received orders assigning me to Fort Jackson, South Carolina, to be an instructor at the Advanced NCO Academy. I didn't want to be an instructor because it wasn't interesting to me. Instead of being an instructor, I went back to the trenches, working at the 5th Basic Training Brigade as the S-1 noncommissioned officer in charge (NCOIC). My duties have been in the personnel arena for nineteen years. Again, I was responsible for all incoming and outgoing personnel, status report changes from duty to hospital, leave, AWOL, temporary duty, and the like. I produced promotion certificates based upon promotion orders, military awards and ceremonies, annual evaluation reports, and the like. My priority was specifically drill sergeants, because the 5th Brigade is a basic training brigade. As luck would have it, I graduated from basic training in this exact brigade. I sentimentally felt as though I came full circle.

After a two-year tour, I left Fort Jackson, South Carolina, and was assigned to a military intelligence (MI) unit in Wackernheim, Germany. I was responsible for the same duties as before. I had to verify financial reports related to military compensation received by the soldiers in my unit. As fate would have it, my commander was fraudulently receiving a basic housing allowance while residing in government quarters! Basic housing allowance is used to pay rent in nongovernment quarters. Following that fiasco, I requested and received an immediate lateral move to the division inspector general's office. The lateral move was to prevent further retaliation from my commander, who was investigated and found to be receiving fraudulent housing benefits. My inspector skills were strong, like spider senses; this job was the bee's knees. This is what the Army trained me to do as part of my obligation, duty, and responsibility. These examples of deceitful practices have been my nemesis. This was the second time I had to verify information against a soldier in receipt of fraudulent benefits they were not entitled to. I received the assignment to the IG office in November 2002, and the Iraq war began in April 2003.

My unit of deployment to Iraq was a division-sized element and was a combined armored division with a headquarters and headquarters company along with two tank companies and two mechanized infantry companies. The size of an Army division is 10,000 to 15,000 personnel, versus a company that is comprised of 130 to 150. I was assigned to Headquarters and Headquarters Company while working for the inspector general's office.

# CHAPTER 3

On May 7, 2003, we boarded contracted buses from Wiesbaden to Landstuhl, Germany. We were manifested for the aircraft, and the body and equipment were weighed. Females were given their "last chance" pregnancy test prior to boarding the direct flight to Kuwait. You are ineligible to deploy if you are found to be pregnant. I would much rather deploy than face eighteen years of parenting challenges at this late age.

The officers in charge of our office at the beginning of the war were Major Mary Fuller (acting inspector general) and Master Sergeant Peter Jefferson, noncommissioned officer in charge (NCOIC). From our six-person office, four female soldiers and two males were selected to deploy. One male was a master sergeant/E-8, MSG Jefferson, and the other was a Department of the Army civilian, Mr. Pelko. Everyone was over forty years old; the rule is that you are soldiers first, mothers, fathers, wives, and husbands second. By the way, this rule is not documented but is true. US soldiers are technically government property; for instance, if a soldier receives a "hickey or passion mark" from their mate or receives a severe sunburn, they will be charged for damage to government property using the manual for court martial, and punishment will be implemented by the officer who administers Article 15, usually your company commander or brigade commander.

After taking the oath of enlistment, you are sworn to defend the constitution against enemies foreign and domestic. The military wasn't very considerate of families during my twenty-two years. I witnessed young mothers hysterically separated from their newborn at six weeks old for duty-related obligations. Now, men and women have received extended maternity leave past the eight-week maternity rule. I couldn't help but pity young and older mothers in this precarious position, and the depression that follows with their children not knowing who they were once redeployed back home has been shared with me on numerous occasions. This is a different type of trauma: time lost with an infant cannot be redeemed.

The enlisted person in charge of three of us women soldiers was Master Sergeant Jefferson. He constantly ranted to anyone who would listen, "*I'm not used to being assigned with females."* He said he was getting a raw deal by deploying to Iraq with four female soldiers without combat experience. He didn't have any combat experience either. His previous assignments were with Air Defense Artillery (ADA) units that were not open to women. I found his banter offensive; we had enough to worry about without being demeaned.

I am sure the master sergeant and the specialist in our office shared an inappropriate relationship; their tents were across from each other, and they were always stuck together like glue. Everywhere we were transported, the master sergeant always sat behind the specialist, offering her personalized security, while all the other three females were on their own. He didn't look out for *all* his soldiers, and that is a written duty for a noncommissioned officer in charge (NCOIC). That is why I believe they were doing hanky-panky.

On April 8, 2014, the Secretary of the Army signed a directive where thirty-three thousand male-only positions and units became open to women, allowing them to enhance their military opportunities, whether in peacetime or war. Female soldiers were not allowed to serve in traditional male-only jobs prior to 2014. Women were not allowed to be in Special Forces units except in support positions such as personnel, cooks, supply, and logistics. It is exciting that women can now choose any military occupational specialty; progress has transpired.

Being an Army administration guru, I knew any request for retirement in 2003 wasn't likely to be approved. So I didn't apply; instead, I was prepared to deploy at forty years old with nineteen years of service. I prayed constantly. I have been a chronic asthmatic since 1989 while stationed in Germany, and going to a dry and dusty climate was dangerous to my condition, but I was medically cleared to deploy. I waited until after deployment to submit for retirement. Based upon the rules of Stop Loss, the Army alone blocked the requested retirements and military moves of more than forty thousand soldiers combined. With these rules in place, there was no reason to request retirement prior to deploying. I knew it would be disapproved, and I would look like a soldier avoiding deployment. I had no extenuating circumstances to support such a request at a time of war. Moreover, such exceptional requests required a one-star general officer endorsement, and who needs that kind of attention?

Being stationed in Germany during an outbreak of war geographically places soldiers in a strategic "staging area," making deployment to any hot spot more expeditious than leaving from the United States.

In April 2003, the Army further issued another stop-loss message: soldiers could not perform any voluntary moves to include retirement. In addition, soldiers Army-wide would cease voluntary movement unless in direct support of the war in Iraq, Operation Iraqi Freedom (OIF).

Our team's job at the inspector general's office was called "the eyes and ears of the Commander." Brigadier General Kevin X. Wilson was our division commander and the ultimate superior in our chain of command after serving as the Army's Army Chief of Staff. Our office interacted with him as our division commander often, and he was a very kind gentleman who genuinely placed the soldier's needs first. Four-Star General Wilson's last assignment was to be the Chairman of the Joint Chiefs of Staff.

After deployment orders were published, my coworkers and I began packing our CONEX shipping container with the necessary office equipment, supplies, and forms needed in Iraq. We prepared our donated Humvee 4-door vehicle with soft doors, performed maintenance prior to shipment, and ordered missing parts to operationalize this vehicle upon delivery in Kuwait. The good Lord told me to go on US

Cavalry's website and invest in my comfort and sanitation items. I purchased a camping shower, which was useless. The water was too hot early in the morning. Take a shower if you wanted to, but you would have third-degree burns afterward. My US Cavalry order included one thousand surgical masks, one thousand surgical gloves, a shit ton of Ziploc quart and gallon bags, Clorox wipes, and body cleaning wipes. I used Ziplocs daily with surgical masks, gloves, and Clorox and antibacterial wipes. It was handy, grab-and-go-to-the-porta-john literally. Soldiers used Ziploc to pack underwear, socks, T-shirts—basically everything we had. We were trained to do that in the event our duffel bags got wet. I always lined my duffel bag with a fifty-gallon trash bag; the contents were in Ziploc bags. I presently use this packing technique minus the duffel bag.

Next, we were issued our desert battle dress uniform (BDU). The uniforms and protective equipment we received were from Desert Shield/Storm 90s. There were suede desert-styled boots identical to Vietnam-era jungle boots. I cannot express how painful walking on three-fourths rocks day in and day out was for me and others—common soldier foot issues. There wasn't enough foot powder to comfort our barking dogs, also known as leather personnel carriers. Upon returning from this deployment, there would be bunion surgeries galore! Including mine; my feet were killing me all the time. I had foot callouses and a right foot bunion. It didn't matter if you had insoles or not; foot pain was abundant. I purchased a wash basin and lots of Epson salt to soak my feet in—aah! What great temporary relief for foot pain!

Our uniforms were made of thick cloth; unfortunately, we didn't have the heat-cooling cloth at this time. In comparison to Iraq, Kuwait was at least twenty degrees cooler. Kuwait is where the first Gulf War occurred in 1990–1991. The daily heat in Iraq was more than 130 degrees. One day, Mr. Pelko and I were smoking cigarettes when we decided to take the digital portable anemometer outside on the rooftop. This location was parallel to the helicopter pad.

The weather station reported 150 degrees that day! My ex-husband didn't believe this is not true, but why would anyone in their right mind exaggerate about 150-degree heat?

The worst part of the day is after you've been on the road all day traveling, and the shower, which is comprised of three thousand-gallon tanks of water, is empty, and you can't take an evening shower. Sleep was hard to come by when you couldn't shower at night. I felt gritty, sweaty, and sticky. The flies and mosquitoes tag-teamed with us. Flies had the day shift, and mosquitoes had a night shift; they were both relentless. I ingested garlic pills, and the mosquitoes happily wanted nothing to do with me. Thankfully, humans couldn't smell the garlic pills, but the intended mosquitoes did. The flies were so aggressive—they wanted moisture, so they flew in your eyes, up your nose, and in your mouth. When we ate at the dining facility, you had to fan with your left hand to eat with your right. It was a repulsive mess that I could not get used to. So many other things were worse than this though.

Additionally, there was another important problem: there wasn't any plumbing in 2003. We relied on port-a-johns as our latrines. When there was a security threat at the front gate, the latrine truck (aka shit-sucking truck) wouldn't be able to enter the base to clean out our port-a-johns; this happened several days a week. I will not explain how graphically nightmarish it was to open the door to the latrine and the poop has exceeded the toilet like a tower.

Horrendous—and the flies!

One positive thing about the unimproved desert BDUs was that the desert camouflage pattern perfectly matched the terrain in Kuwait and Iraq. Our outdated green protective flak jackets (bulletproof vests) were issued before departing Germany. In 2003, we deployed to Iraq with one metal plate per soldier versus the standard set of two metal plates per soldier. There weren't enough plates for every soldier to receive two. Every day's life-or-death challenge was deciding whether to put the metal plate in the front or back of the vest. If you rode shotgun passenger as I did, I always had my plate in the front, and my rear passenger had their plate in the back of their vest. I never had a warm and fuzzy feeling about how safe I felt during this deployment. Everyone's head was on swivel all the time. We were tense all the time, day and night. During the day, the local Iraqis fought for day work on the base, and at night we received mortar fire in our camps that was so dangerous. I don't recall anyone dying because of mortar fatalities, which doesn't mean it didn't happen. However, I knew someone who was literally blown out of his bunk while sleeping. We had sandbags on the outside of our tents all the way around; the height of them was approximately five feet high. Every part of his tent was literally blown away except the five-foot lower part of his tent, reinforced with sandbags.

The Armored Division HHC element arrived in Kuwait on May 8, 2003. We lived in camps given names such as Camp Pennsylvania and Camp New York. In Kuwait, soldiers went to Finance to have our hostile fire/danger pay, hazardous duty pay, family separation pay, basic allowance for sustenance, pay for food, and basic housing allowance started for families back home for rent and utilities. The personnel portion was to ensure that our life insurance was unequivocally correct in the event of our death. Importantly, you must know that some soldiers were married when we did our pre-deployment processing before leaving Germany but were divorced by the time we were boots on the ground in the deployment country. We also had to receive our vehicles (Humvee, with soft doors) shipped by train and sealift. Once our team's vehicle was received, the parts shipped inside the vehicle were installed while at the port of Kuwait. Following the repairs, there was a huge relief: we ordered all the right parts, and our vehicle was operational. We finally had our own transportation. Our office didn't have an assigned military vehicle; we didn't have a need for it in Germany. There, we transported fifteen passenger vans and government sedans.

To reach the facility in Kuwait from our living area on Camp Pennsylvania, you had to trek through the hot-ass desert for an approximate half-mile round trip. The daily lunch menu was published at breakfast. All day, you are hyped up, thinking you are having stuffed barnyard pimp (chicken)! The menu changes without your knowledge to hot dogs and hamburgers. This "reality" is why I wouldn't go to the dining facility. One day, Master Sergeant Jefferson and Mr. Pelko walked over to the dining facility, ate, and returned to our group tent. I was taking a nap, and this bothered Mr. Pelko; he initiated an argument about why I was taking a nap during lunchtime. My response was "What better time to rest the body from the heat instead of going into the heat for a crappy meal?" It escalated to being in each other's faces, and we almost did the Ali shuffle.

The good old NCOIC just watched instead of de-escalating the tiff. Another bad check on him, in my opinion. Taking a nap during lunch in 140-plus heat is not forbidden. From 1130 to 1300 was our lunchtime. If you wanted to stand on your head for an hour and a half, that was your business. I took my chances with the Meals Ready to Eat or MREs (aka "Meals Requiring Enemas," "Meals Refusing to Exit," "Meals Refusing to Excrete," and lastly, "Massive Rectal Expulsions"). Their low dietary fiber content causes these "stick around" memes. MREs are scientifically designed to go in and not come out!

Their purpose is to not allow the enemy to follow your unit's defecation habits. Because of my dining choice, I was later diagnosed with IBS-C, or irritable bowel syndrome with Constipation.

During 2003, ice cream contractors couldn't guarantee the delivery of ice cream. It was the craziest experience I ever saw; soldiers were happy to drink their ice cream though. I also chose not to eat red meat (beef or pork) or chicken loaf. I never saw any farm animals, and any food in a loaf is mystery meat, in my opinion. By eliminating meat, I was not very energetic, so I ate a lot of toast with peanut butter and bananas for breakfast, beans, salad, and tuna fish. When given a choice during our 1130 to 1300 lunch break, I chose to rest. It was too hot and far to walk for the consumption of disappointment. Instead, I always conserved my hydration and energy by taking a lunchtime nap for one and a half hours. Eventually, the base post exchange opened, and they had great choices of pogey bait (e.g., junk food). The PX could be described as a metal container turned into a store with no windows and sweltering heat. The military has been using the term pogey bait as early as 1918. Our meals had two offerings of MREs (Meals Ready to Eat). MREs weren't bad, but they didn't taste like real food. The dining facility served hot dogs and hamburgers, or this disgusting fish filet that was blackened. So spicy; I desired it but couldn't eat it. They served it five days out of seven.

We stayed in Kuwait for roughly a month, May–June 2003, and it was hot as Hades. We finally left Kuwait late in the day and drove most of the night; I can't remember the date in June. When we stopped to sleep, we slept on the hoods of our vehicles because of snakes and camel spiders. HHC convoyed vehicles from Kuwait to Iraq in twenty-two hours. I drove our vehicle the entire twenty-two-hour trip. One of the times we took a latrine break, the division surgeon passed out these pills to help us stay awake. If I were to make an educated guess, I would say he gave us medical methamphetamine. Whatever that pill was, I didn't sleep for three consecutive days.

# CHAPTER 4

**W**e finally arrived in Iraq in the evening of the next day. Our quarters were at the Baghdad International Airport, located about twenty miles from downtown Baghdad. I would put my uniform on in the morning, and by the time we returned from that day's mission, my uniform was covered with sweat from hair to foot. The sweaty days were when we had to leave Baghdad International Airport (BIAP) to visit other subordinate units assigned to our division. Our IG team drove to different units around Baghdad to assess soldiers' living conditions; we provided solutions to improve the soldier's quality of life. Life in Iraq was bad enough without flea infestations in the living areas. Examples of our day's mission were:

- A company commander was often sighting the laser of his weapon on an African American soldier's chest. We received a handwritten note regarding this infraction; the soldier was too afraid to report the incident in person. Following the investigation and witness statements, the company commander, a CPT, was relieved of his duties.

- A lieutenant colonel allowed all female officers in his battalion to play volleyball dressed in their sports bras and Army physical training shorts. Sports bras are not an authorized part of Army physical training uniform. The Army PT uniform consisted of an Army T-shirt in gray, shorts in black, and a jacket in gray with a black stripe. Anything other than what was described was not authorized for wear.
- The most significant media event within our division was the Abu Gharib prison scandal in 2004.

When leaving the base, we wore 210 bullets in seven, thirty-round magazines, and a backpack with needed items weighing around fifty pounds. We worked six days a week, twelve hours a day. Truthfully, that was fine for me. Iraq was the only war zone I have ever deployed to in my nineteen years of service. There wasn't a need to know the day or the date when *indefinite* was your return date. The only exception was writing a check, preparing written correspondence, or your day of departure. Wouldn't want to miss that!

On the seventh day, we hand-washed and hung out a week's worth of clothes. One time early in the deployment, we hung our clothes out overnight to dry, and a sandstorm (haboob) came in the middle of the night. So the clothes had to be washed after work because we weren't successful on our day off. Two things could happen when hanging out clothes:

1. a haboob (sandstorm), or
2. someone stole your uniforms or underwear because they didn't have enough.

After the haboob incident, an adjustment was established. Wash them early on your day off, and hang them out early. It only took approximately one hour to dry. I read 160 books during my deployment, thanks to my HP Personal Data Assistant (PDA). I had five thousand songs and numerous Kindle books to occupy my time while washing my clothes.

I can attest to seeing certain soldiers during breakfast, and by dinnertime, they were in a body bag. There was a disturbing incident involving a particular soldier who wandered away from his unit and went inside this building at Baghdad International Airport (BIAP) called "Hotel California."

This soldier was reportedly eighteen years old and fresh out of basic training and Advanced Individual Training (AIT), where you learn the technical part of your job. He committed suicide with his M16 rifle. His body wasn't discovered for at least forty-eight hours. When he was found, the heat had decomposed his body so rapidly—it was so sad. Our chaplain told us about it over dinner. I can't get this story out of my mind years after leaving Iraq. Soldiers were often in Iraq for twelve months after swearing their lives and allegiance to join the military. I am indicating their level of life experience was zero to nil. Letters from home at that time were delivered to Iraq thirty to ninety days after they were mailed. Mail was the juice that every soldier needs, so the telephone lines were extremely long every day. Sundays were worse. Standing in line is something everyone does every day. There were lines for the phones; our office had a satellite phone, which was a savior. I didn't talk to my family the whole time I was in Iraq. I couldn't burden my mind and be off my head-swivel game. I did call my sister-in-law because we are so close; all she did was cry. I never called anyone after that episode. I couldn't afford anything that shifted my mind. We have a saying: *stay alert, stay alive.*

# CHAPTER 5

The day before the ambush, SPC Lorenze's Humvee mirror bracket was too high for her four-foot, ten-inch height. MSG Jefferson adjusted the mirror bracket lower to offer her better visibility.

Also, the night before *that* day, I was spiritually inclined to read 108 pages of Proverbs in my Bible. There are thirty-one chapters in the book of Proverbs. Following this reading, I felt temporarily uplifted; my soul no longer felt so weary from mental and physical exhaustion. My relationship with God is steadfast. I wholeheartedly believe that Jesus is my savior who died on the cross for my sins. After that reading, my mind played out a questionable scenario: what would happen if SPC Lorenze was injured while driving the Humvee?

I worked out how I would snatch her into the back seat and climb over the console to drive us to safety. I got it. That is what I will do if that situation arises.

# CHAPTER 6

*T**hat day*, after breakfast on July 3, 2003, we attend our mandatory convoy briefing at 0800 and receive instructions on what actions to execute *if* we are involved in an ambush. The division's force protection assessment team provides vehicle escorts for us and every vehicle convoy departing from the Baghdad International Airport (BIAP) location.

Following the briefing, we mount our vehicles and depart BIAP. We were traveling to conduct a site survey of the 12th of the 64th Infantry Battalion. A site survey is a sampling of the unit's population and morale. As investigators, we ask different ranking soldiers of that unit what they are struggling with and how these struggles can be best improved. Their location was on the other side of downtown Baghdad.

That day was not the same as any other day. I was later told I acted with intense hypervigilance. For example, previously, I didn't make it a habit to lock and load my M-16 before we crossed the barrels. The barrels are what separates BIAP from outside the perimeter enemy zone. Before this day, I was not in a rush; usually, I would lock and load *after* passing the barrels.

That day, I locked and loaded *before* crossing the barrels. Nothing was funny that day; there was no joking like usual. I had a very weird feeling, and I felt as if I *knew* something was going to happen that day.

# CHAPTER 7

**O**n July 3, 2003, at approximately 0900, SPC Lorenze was driving, and I was the truck commander (TC). I sat in the front passenger seat while traveling. Again, coordination of your "plate" is crucial. I know I wasn't alone in this thought. That day, I experienced a sort of static-electric feeling of impending doom. I couldn't be comfortable; everyone was on swivel and pucker power. After the convoy briefing, we depart from BIAP in a three-vehicle convoy.

This trip required us to travel through the downtown outdoor market. There are so many people in the market that three soldiers dismount per vehicle to walk alongside the vehicle, therefore providing effective perimeter protection for our vehicle while traveling at this creeping, crawling speed of two miles per hour. We depart the market with a huge sigh of relief. After mounting our assigned vehicles, we continue to travel toward downtown Baghdad. Haifa Street was the most direct route to reach the 12th of the 64th Infantry Battalion. The downside is that Haifa Street held a strategic disadvantage for American soldiers and was notorious for ambush attacks. After passing through the crowded traffic circle, which is four-lanes deep, we were inside, and both lanes merged onto Haifa Street. Haifa Street is all high-rise buildings. Haifa Street is also known as Purple Heart Alley.

My job is to observe all vehicles in every situation. As we were rounding this traffic circle, beside us, there was an older Iraqi woman in the passenger seat of her vehicle. It is so hard to determine Iraqis ages because the sun has prematurely ages Iraqi's skin. Our eyes met, and she gave me the thumbs-up sign and the biggest childish grin; she had gold teeth. My interpretation is: *You go, girl. We can't do anything like that as an Iraqi woman.* I had an intense feeling of pride being a US soldier. Experiencing immense pride in being a soldier in battle dress and of our driver also being female. Driving in Baghdad was akin to driving in Egypt. SPC Lorenze was a strong soldier, and because she was only four-feet tall, she never backed down from any assignment she was given. She and I always said that when things got tough, we were some *BBs (bad b******)*.

Being a soldier on foreign soil during an armed conflict takes guts, believe me—King Kong–sized guts.

At 0900, insurgents attacked our vehicle from the rooftop of a high-rise building. The insurgents saw us coming for at least ten miles before we were under attack. Our group was a three-vehicle convoy with two gunners (people stationed in an elevated position in the center of the vehicle). We traveled without doors, using headlights as was mandatory, per convoy procedures. The lack of doors offered no protection from the IEDs explosions. I believe the scariest thing is when you don't know where you're going except by map, and you don't know what will happen on the way.

Once on Haifa Street, I noticed a strange anomaly: on both sides of the sidewalk, there were a huge number of civilians lining the street. They look at us as if they know something is about to happen. I said to myself, *Hmm…why are there so many people out at 0900? Maybe there is a parade coming?* That is when I heard the whistle of the rocket-propelled grenade from the high-rise rooftop, which detonated a civilian vehicle containing bombs. That car explodes and detonates three daisy chain munitions, also known as IEDs (improvised explosive device). The IEDs exploded under vehicle 1, in front of vehicle 2, and in front of vehicle 3. The vehicle went up into the air with passengers and slammed back down on the concrete, exploding all four tires. The explosion shook me to the core, sending heat from the top of my head to the bottom of my feet. It felt like something internal caused everything to be in slow motion, hearing that loud screeching hum in my ears while feeling disoriented and dazed. During this chaos, I am thinking, *This must be what an out-of-body experience may feel like.* It was raining debris, asphalt, screws, and all kinds of makeshift metal particles so badly that it took a while to see our hands before our faces. The feeling internally was like a seismic earthquake times four. The waves of the explosion were later very traumatizing. While this is happening, you are one step behind the action until it is felt. We were coated in the dust, making visibility impossible. The dust was especially in our eyes. Also, we were bombarded by the same group of insurgents now using AK-47 rifles. I heard a high-pitched screeching ringing in my ear following the blasts because my eardrum was pierced, and I have neurological hearing loss. The bone that conducts hearing was damaged because of the impact of the explosions.

During the follow-on attack, one bullet came into my passenger window and traveled between four passenger shoulders. Humvee windows are single panels; if I or either of us had turned our heads, this story would not be written.

The insurgents initially fired one rocket-propelled grenade (RPG[1]), detonating a car bomb[2]. The car bomb detonated a daisy chain of three IEDs[3] and an improvised explosive device (IED[3]) (the superscript numbers indicate five successive munition attacks). The first IED exploded directly beneath the lead convoy Humvee, blowing it off the asphalt and slamming the truck on the ground, exploding all four tires. The occupants were MP escorts, mixed with 5th AD sergeant major and master sergeant. That disabled vehicle forced five of its passengers to evacuate into the crowd of spectators. My vehicle was the second vehicle; three passengers were from the 5th AD inspector general's office, and the fourth passenger I'd never seen before, nor since was a part of the MP escort. We had an empty seat, so he filled it. The third vehicle driver was struck by the same AK-47 bullet that entered my window, lodging in the lip of his Kevlar helmet. If he had worn his helmet in the "John Wayne" style, where the front is kicked up, he surely would have been dead. The raining asphalt and being shot in the head caused him to reflectively smash on the gas. Our second vehicle was rear-ended and entangled in the third vehicle's bumper. A chunk of our rear driver's side bumper was torn out while freeing our vehicle during this firefight.

Here is a blurb about our ambush on July 3, 2003, from the Reuters newspaper:

> *The violence reached a zenith on July 3, when a patrol was ambushed on Haifa Street, the main thoroughfare in Karkh, by Iraqis who fired a rocket-propelled grenade at a Humvee and then opened fire with automatic weapons. Three U.S. troops were wounded, two Iraqi bystanders were killed in the crossfire, and 14 were injured.* (Reuters)

Thankfully, non–life-threatening injuries were sustained by everyone involved in this convoy, and there were no fatalities. I count this as a blessing and am so grateful for the outcome. If you remember, there were five soldiers forced to dismount their vehicles. During our convoy briefing, we were told that if attacked, we would leave the kill zone and regroup. We did exactly that; in the process, we had to leave those five soldiers on Haifa Street, who took shelter under the balcony of a first-floor apartment. We rounded the block in the remaining vehicles of the convoy, assessing our damages, and returned back to Haifa Street to the area where we were attacked and quickly retrieved our soldiers. I remember being so inwardly afraid to return to Haifa Street, but it was a necessary act.

Thankfully, my driver, SPC Lorenze, survived the attack and wasn't injured. I didn't have to use yesterday's scenario. Later, we see lodged in the newly adjusted mirror bracket a massive piece of shrapnel that would have penetrated the left side of her chest. The mirror adjustment MSG Jefferson made the day before saved her life. The IED incident rocked my world from then until now. I am involved in an eight-year fight with the Veterans Administration regarding a closed head injury that they say doesn't exist because there was no report written and placed in my personnel files. I am writing to the Board of Military Corrections. I am in the process of getting a sworn statement from my company commander. Arduous processes are common when trying to get the benefits you are so deserving of. I call this systemic abuse; benefits delayed are benefits lost.

MSG Jefferson and I were the only two people of fourteen who returned suppressive fire to dissuade the insurgents from massacring us. We created a diversion that saved many lives that day.

Sad to say that during this firefight, two small girls were killed in the process of defending our convoy with suppressive fire. It wasn't until about two years ago that I could finally let this tragedy go for my own mental well-being. A veteran counselor I went to at the VA explained to me that I didn't ask to be there and it was not intentional. Thirdly, why did their parents have them out there in the first place? I couldn't have discerned this on my own because of survivors' guilt, and seeing those two girls in their pretty dresses as they were piled in a taxi van while being rushed to the hospital is seared into my mind. The taxi van was right next to where I was standing. My heart sank because I knew they were likely our kills. I will never forget this day as long as I live. I still go through so many emotions just writing this part. There was an irony to this incident. My deceased mother's birthday is July 3, 1944. I believe God deflected the bullets and my mother was my angel that day.

We resumed traveling throughout Iraq a month later, and for the six remaining months, I was in Iraq. After the ambush, we continued to see soldiers at their location.

Our office continued to drive to different units around Baghdad to assess soldiers living conditions; we continued to provide solutions to improve the soldiers' quality of life.

# CHAPTER 8

I became sick with pneumonia again in Baghdad on January 16, 2004, six months after the ambush. My asthma, the dust, and daily burn-pit exposure made breathing impossible that day. I tried taking cold medicine, but my severe breathing symptoms persisted. My temperature was over 105 Fahrenheit, I was feverish, and my chest was so tight, so I used our vehicle and drove myself to the small medical clinic for treatment. Everyone else in the office was at lunch. I was medevaced to a field hospital on January 16, and I was further medevaced to Germany on January 18, 2004. I was returned to duty and went to work that same day I returned to Germany. Everyone in my office who deployed was awarded the Bronze Star, except the one who was medevaced (me) because I didn't spend six more months in Iraq. I have come to a resolution: the loss of a Bronze Star is a small price to pay.

My life after this incident has been a painful journey in many aspects. I volunteer and help other veterans of all eras receive their benefits. I am involved in three veteran organizations where we do good deeds for my community. I am very happy with where I am. I am eternally grateful every day for the life I have, although I work daily to improve it. I pray for every soldier who has night terrors and night sweats and is suffering from the aftereffects of war or peace. The VA has recently approved assistance for military sexual trauma (MST) victims; this is a wonderful move in the right direction. Many female soldiers were raped and sexually assaulted in earlier eras of service. They have had to live with that incident without VA assistance. I am so glad that they can now get the help they need to overcome the stigma and embarrassment of their incident.

I continue with my video therapy, and it falls so short of effective treatment. It has been so long since I have had a face-to-face therapist that I cannot even tell you the year. I continue to fight for myself and other veterans who have fallen through the cracks of VA health and VA benefits. That is the cape I have come to wear, and it feels good to my soul. Helping is my forte. My granny always said *if you can't help a person, be resourceful enough to guide them in the right direction.* I do live by that.

As far as relationships, I am not involved in one at the moment. However, I hope the right person will come along and understand my wounded body and mind. Until then, I must continue to fight the systemic bureaucracy for others while I cannot help myself attain my benefits. That is what helps me heal.

After the 5 explosions debris is in the street

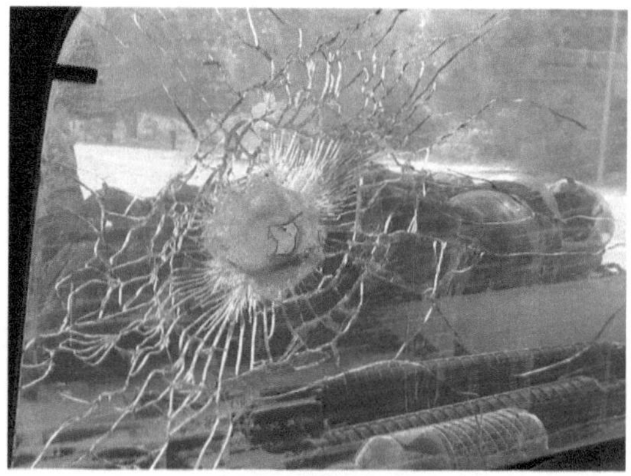

Bullet hole #1

Vehicle of Driver #3 Bullet hole #1

Driver #3 With treated injuries from Bullet #1

Driver #3's Kevlar Helmet with AK47 entry hole

Driver #3 vehicle with bumper panel torn off

AK47 bullet graze on Passenger in #1 Vehicle Kevlar

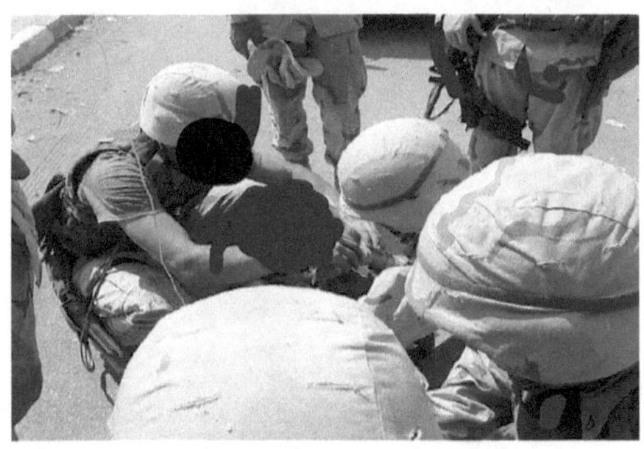

Medics stabilizing patient

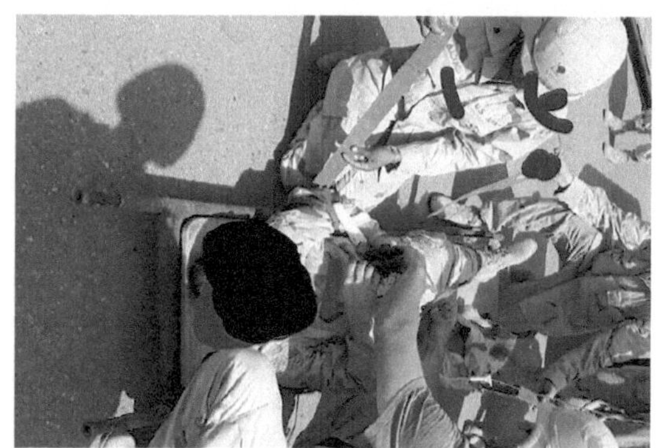

Medics preparing patient for medivac

SPC Lorenze's adjusted brack

Vehicle #2 SPC Lorenze's bracket with
schrapnel embedded in the bracket

Vehicle #1 disabled before we departed

U.S. Army vehicle after it was hit by
a rocket-propelled grenade

SUPPORT OUR TROOPS

Iraqi men and children celebrate as they tear apart a
U.S. Army vehicle after it was hit by a rocket-propelled
grenade in Baghdad, July 3, 2003. At least one U.S.
soldier and two Iraqi passers-by were wounded in the
attack on Thursday and in a separate incident another
six U.S. soldiers were wounded in western Iraq (news
- web sites) in the latest of spate of increasingly bold
guerrilla-style attacks. REUTERS/Faleh Kheiber

Vehicle #1 after we departed

Setting up a perimeter after returning from regroup

Return from regrouping and assessing damage

Return from regrouping and assessing damage

The surviving group minus two medical evacuees

# ABOUT THE AUTHOR

Tasha is a passionate ghostwriter specializing in military memoirs, dedicated to capturing the stories of service members and their journeys with loyalty and a deep admiration for the sacrifices and experiences of those who have served. Tasha combines a background in creative writing with a twenty-three-year understanding of military culture and history.

Drawing on her own experience as an active-duty combat soldier serving during the 2003–2004 period of Operation Iraqi Freedom in Baghdad, Iraq, Tasha crafts compelling and authentic narratives that honor the voices of veterans, active-duty personnel, and their families. Her approach is characterized by empathy, attention to detail, and a commitment to preserving the integrity of everyone's story.

Tasha holds a bachelor's and a master's degree and has developed a unique writing style that merges engaging storytelling with meticulous research. Tasha continues to collaborate with various veteran and military organizations to create impactful content that educates, inspires, and enlivens the experiences of those who have served. Tasha is actively seeking new projects and partnerships to bring military stores to life, in hopes of one day reaching the silver screen.

When not immersed in writing, she can be found volunteering with different veteran assistance programs, assisting veterans with filing claims and getting the benefits they deserve. Tasha is also a crochet clothes designer.